Your Piggy Bank:
A **Guide** to **Spending**
& Saving for **Kids!**

MONEY
······· FOR ·······
SCHOOL

magic
wagon

MARY ELIZABETH SALZMANN

**Consulting Editor, Diane Craig,
M.A./Reading Specialist**

**Paula Austin, B.A. Elementary
Education/Math Consultant**

visit us at www.abdopublishing.com

Published by Magic Wagon, a division of the ABDO Group,
8000 West 78th Street, Edina, Minnesota 55439.

Copyright © 2011 by Abdo Consulting Group, Inc. International copyrights reserved in all countries.

Printed in the United States of America, North Mankato, Minnesota .
062010
092010

 This book contains at least 10% recycled materials.

Editor: Katherine Hengel
Content Developer: Nancy Tuminelly

Library of Congress Cataloging-in-Publication Data

Salzmann, Mary Elizabeth, 1968-
 Money for school / by Mary Elizabeth Salzmann.
   p. cm. -- (Your piggy bank: a guide to spending & saving for kids!)
 ISBN 978-1-61641-031-5
 1. Money--Juvenile literature. 2. Student activities--Costs--Juvenile literature. 3. Schools--Costs--Juvenile literature.
 4. Mathematics--Juvenile literature. I. Title.
 HG221.5.S266 2011
 332.024--dc22
                       2009053780

What About Tax?

Given the audience and nature of this series, we chose not to directly address taxes as an element of an item's price. For the purposes of this series, the taxes are included in the prices!

CONTENTS

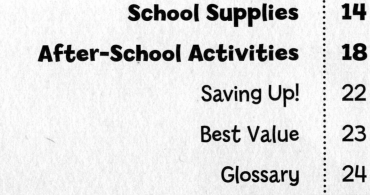

COINS AND BILLS

PENNY		**ONE CENT**	1¢ or $0.01
NICKEL		**FIVE CENTS**	5¢ or $0.05
DIME		**TEN CENTS**	10¢ or $0.10
QUARTER		**TWENTY-FIVE CENTS**	25¢ or $0.25
DOLLAR BILL		**ONE DOLLAR** equal to one hundred cents	100¢ or $1.00

More Coins

There are also coins worth fifty cents and one dollar.

More Bills

Some bills are worth more than one dollar. Look for the number in the corners of a bill. That is how many dollars the bill is worth.

SPENDING MONEY

Here are some important ideas to think about when spending money.

Price
The price is how much you pay for something.

Quantity
The quantity is how many things you buy.

Quality
The quality of something is how well it is made or how well it works.

Value
Value is how price, quantity, and quality work together. It is good to think about value before you buy something.

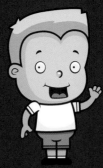

Meet Mason!
Mason's parents give him money. He gets to decide what to buy. Follow along with Mason as he tries to make good decisions.

Mason's Goal
Mason wants to buy a new backpack. It costs $12.50. His **goal** is to save enough money to buy the backpack.

Mason's Savings
Mason puts his savings in his piggy bank. He saves a little bit at a time. Small amounts can add up to a lot!

FIELD TRIP

Mason's class is going to a petting zoo. Mason loves to feed the animals! His parents give him some bills and coins. How much money did they give him?

Organize the bills and coins into groups. Then add the groups together.

Find the total of each group. Then add the group totals together.

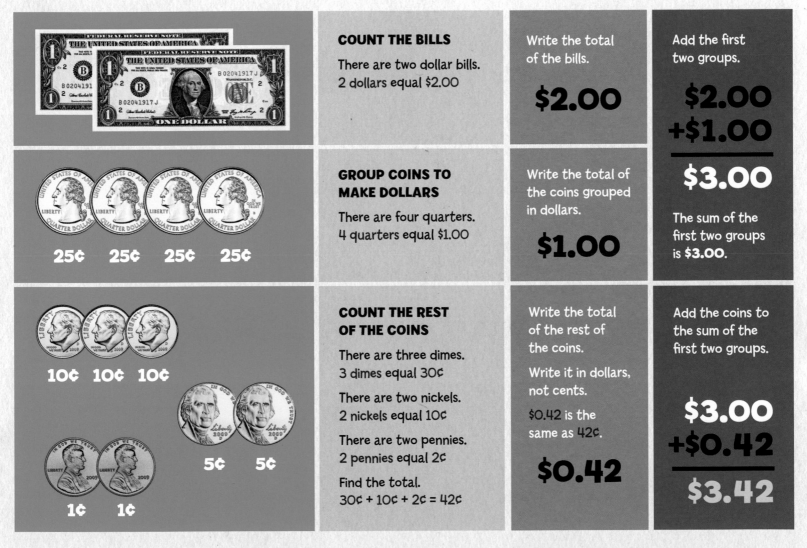

COUNT THE BILLS

There are two dollar bills. 2 dollars equal $2.00

Write the total of the bills.

$2.00

Add the first two groups.

$2.00 +$1.00

$3.00

GROUP COINS TO MAKE DOLLARS

There are four quarters. 4 quarters equal $1.00

25¢ 25¢ 25¢ 25¢

Write the total of the coins grouped in dollars.

$1.00

The sum of the first two groups is **$3.00**.

COUNT THE REST OF THE COINS

There are three dimes. 3 dimes equal 30¢

There are two nickels. 2 nickels equal 10¢

There are two pennies. 2 pennies equal 2¢

Find the total. 30¢ + 10¢ + 2¢ = 42¢

10¢ 10¢ 10¢

5¢ 5¢

1¢ 1¢

Write the total of the rest of the coins.

Write it in dollars, not cents.

$0.42 is the same as 42¢.

$0.42

Add the coins to the sum of the first two groups.

$3.00 +$0.42

$3.42

The total amount of all the bills and coins is **$3.42**.

Add It Up!

Mason's parents gave him **$3.42** to buy animal feed. Then the teacher gave each student **$1.00**. Now how much money does Mason have?

> I did the math on a piece of paper. You can see how I did it below. The total is **$4.42**.

Do the Math

Adding decimal numbers is a lot like adding whole numbers.

Line up the decimal points.

$3.42
+$1.00
———

Start from the right and add each column.

$3.42
+$1.00
———
2

Put a decimal point in the answer. It goes below the other decimal points.

$3.42
+$1.00
———
$4.42

Include the dollar sign in the answer.

Do the Math

Subtracting decimal numbers is a lot like subtracting whole numbers.

Line up the decimal points.

$4.42
- $3.32

Start from the right and subtract each column.

$4.42
- $3.32
0

Put a decimal point in the answer. It goes below the other decimal points.

$4.42
- $3.32
$1.10

Include the dollar sign in the answer.

Subtract It!

Mason has **$4.42**. He buys a bag of feed that costs **$3.32**. How much money does Mason have left?

Mason had **$4.42**. He spent **$3.32**. Now he has **$1.10**. Mason puts the leftover money into his piggy bank.

I'll have $1.10 left to put in my piggy bank! You can see how I figured it out at the top of the page.

Mason's Piggy Bank

$0.00
+$1.10
$1.10

SCHOOL LUNCH

Mason is buying lunch. He needs to buy a main dish and a drink. He can spend **$4.00** or less.

What should Mason buy?

$2.50

$3.50

$4.00

$0.50

$1.60

$2.00

Do the Math

Some of the food and drink combinations cost more than **$4.00**. Let's look at a couple of examples.

$2.50 + $2.00 = $4.50

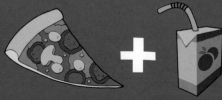

$3.50 + $1.60 = $5.10

Decision Time

Mason has two **options**. He can buy the pizza with the milk. Or, he can buy the sandwich with milk. All the other combinations cost too much.

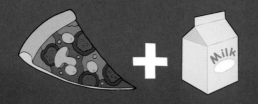

$3.50 + $0.50 = $4.00

$2.50 + $0.50 = $3.00

If Mason buys the pizza with the milk, he will spend all his money. If he buys the sandwich with the milk, he will still have a dollar!

I'm going to have the sandwich and the milk. Then I'll have $1.00 left to put in my piggy bank!

Mason had **$4.00**. He spent $3.00. Now he has **$1.00**. Mason puts the leftover money into his piggy bank.

Mason's Piggy Bank

$1.10
+$1.00
―――――
$2.10

Add It Up!

Mason wants to buy a snack. The carrots cost **$0.95**. The dip costs **$0.23**. What is the total cost?

$0.95 $0.23

I figured it out! It was easier when I wrote it down on paper. The total cost is **$1.18**.

Do the Math	Line up the decimal points.	Start from the right and add each column.	Regroup when digits in a column total ten or more.	Write the decimal point in the answer.
Adding decimal numbers is a lot like adding whole numbers.	$0.95 +$0.23	$0.95 +$0.23 ——— 8	1 $0.95 +$0.23 ——— 18	$0.95 +$0.23 ——— $1.18

Do the Math

Subtracting decimal numbers is a lot like subtracting whole numbers.

Line up the decimal points.

$2.09
- $1.18
_____

Start from the right and subtract each column.

$2.09
- $1.18
_____
      1

Regroup as you would when subtracting whole numbers.

  1 10
$~~2~~.09
- $1.18
_____
     91

Write the decimal point in the answer.

$2.09
- $1.18
_____
 $0.91

Subtract It!

I'll have $0.91 left to put in my piggy bank! You can see how I figured it out at the top of the page.

Mason's parents give him **$2.09** to buy a snack. Mason knows that the total cost is **$1.18**. How much money will he have left?

Mason had **$2.09**. He spent **$1.18**. Now he has **$0.91**. Mason puts the leftover money into his piggy bank.

Mason's Piggy Bank

$2.10
+$0.91
_____
$3.01

SCHOOL SUPPLIES

Mason is buying pencils for the school year. He can spend **$5.00** or less. Which pack should he buy?

$4.25

$4.25

$4.25

Think About It

To get the best value, he needs to think about price and quantity.

PRICE

All of the packs of pencils are the same price.

QUANTITY

The pack of yellow pencils has 20 pencils.
The pack of colorful pencils has 10 pencils.
The pack of superhero pencils has 5 pencils.

Decision Time

Mason can afford any of the pencil packs. But he needs enough pencils for the whole year.

YELLOW PENCILS

There are 20 pencils in the pack of yellow pencils. Mason knows he would have enough for the whole year.

COLORFUL PENCILS

Mason thinks it would be nice to have colorful pencils. But he doesn't think 10 pencils will be enough.

SUPERHERO PENCILS

Mason would love to have superhero pencils. But he knows that 5 pencils will only last a few weeks.

The yellow pencils are the best value. The other packs may be better looking. But they wouldn't last the whole year.

> I'm going to buy the pack of yellow pencils. It's a better deal because I'll get more pencils for the same price.

Mason had **$5.00**. He spent **$4.25**. Now he has **$0.75**. Mason puts the leftover money into his piggy bank.

Mason's Piggy Bank

$3.01
+$0.75
———
$3.76

THE GIRL WHO HAD NO PENCILS

Mason chose the pack of yellow pencils. Mason thought it was the best value. Mason's friend Alana made a different decision. She chose the superhero pencils. Who made the best decision? Let's see what happens!

Hi, Mason! I can't wait to show you my superhero pencils! They're the coolest pencils ever! What kind did you buy?

I got the yellow pencils. They seemed like the best value.

BORING! *My* pencils are SO much cooler than *yours*! WHO CARES that you got more pencils for the same price?

It looks like Mason made the best decision. And now he has an extra cookie to show for it!

AFTER-SCHOOL ACTIVITIES

Mason is buying **cleats** for the soccer season. He can spend **$20.00** or less. Which cleats should Mason buy?

$5.50

$20.00

$10.00

Think About It

To get the best value, he needs to think about price and quality.

PRICE

The blue cleats have the lowest price. The red cleats have the highest price.

QUALITY

The red cleats look the toughest. They have the best quality. The blue cleats look the least sturdy. They have the worst quality.

Decision Time

Mason can afford any of the cleats. He thinks about each pair's price and quality.

THE BLUE CLEATS

The blue cleats have the lowest price. But they also have the worst quality. They would save Mason the most money. But they might not last the whole season.

THE RED CLEATS

The red cleats have the best quality. But they also have the highest price. They would last a long time. But he would have to spend all his money.

THE GREEN CLEATS

The green cleats have a low price *and* good quality. Mason won't have to spend all his money, *and* they'll last a long time.

The blue **cleats** aren't tough enough for Mason. He doesn't like their quality.

The red cleats are too expensive. Mason doesn't want to spend that much.

He thinks the green cleats look pretty sturdy. And they don't cost a lot!

I'm going to buy the green cleats. Then I'll have $10.00 to put in my piggy bank!

Mason had **$20.00**. He spent **$10.00**. Now he has **$10.00**. Mason puts the leftover money into his piggy bank.

Mason's Piggy Bank

$3.76
+$10.00
$13.76

THE CASE OF THE BROKEN CLEATS

Choosing the cheapest thing isn't always the best idea. Usually, the less something costs, the worse its quality is. Saving money might not be worth it if what you buy doesn't last.

Mason chose better **cleats** than David. He scored a **goal**, and he gets to play in the playoffs!

SAVING UP!

Mason's **goal** was to buy a backpack for **$12.50**. He saved a little bit of money at a time. Finally, he was able to buy the backpack! He is proud of himself for making good buying decisions.

Mason saved **$13.76**. He saved enough money to buy the backpack!

BEST VALUE

Remember that value is a combination of price, quantity, and quality. You usually can't have the best of all three. You have to decide which is most important. If you think about value, you will make good buying decisions.

SHOP AT DOLLAR STORES

Dollar stores can have great deals on school supplies. When price is important, a dollar store is a good place to start.

BUY IN BULK

Buying in bulk means buying a lot of something at once. You can often get a better price when you buy a large quantity.

BUY USED ITEMS

Garage sales and **thrift stores** are good places to find deals. You can sometimes find high quality items for low prices.

GLOSSARY

cleat – 1. a shoe with metal or rubber points on the sole to provide traction. 2. a metal or rubber point on the bottom of a shoe.

garage – a room or building that cars are kept in. A garage sale is a sale that takes place in a garage.

goal – 1. something you try to get or accomplish. 2. a point scored for getting an object into a goal.

option – something you can choose.

organize – to arrange things in a certain way.

thrift store – a store that sells used items, especially one that is run by a charity.